ABUNDANT TRUTH INTERNATIONAL MINISTRIES

Abundant Truth Leadership Series

The Gideon Guide

Biblical Lessons in Leadership from God's "Man of Valor"

Roderick Levi Evans

The Gideon Guide

Biblical Lessons in Leadership from God's "Man of Valor"

All Rights Reserved © 2025 by Roderick L. Evans

No part of this book may be reproduced or transmitted in any form or by any means, graphic, electronic, or mechanical, including photocopying, recording, taping or by any information storage or retrieval system, without permission in writing from the publisher. Front & Back Cover Designs by Abundant Truth Publishing

Front & Back Cover Designs by Abundant Truth International Publishing
Image by CallaNegra from Pixabay

Abundant Truth Publishing
an imprint of Abundant Truth International Ministries
For information address:
Abundant Truth International
P.O. Box 126
Camden, NC 27921

ISBN 13: 978-1-60141-677-3

Printed in the United States of America

Unless otherwise indicated, all of the scripture quotations are taken from the *Authorized King James Version* of the Bible. Scripture quotations marked with NIV are taken from the *New International Version* of the Bible. Scripture quotations marked with NASV are taken from the *New American Standard Version* of the Bible. Scripture quotations marked with Amplified are taken from the *Amplified Bible*.

Contents

Introduction

Chapter 1 – Gideon's Self Perception   1
Personal Perception   *3*
Leadership Mandate   *4*

Chapter 2 – Gideon's Example Obedience   9
Gideons' Name   *11*
Gideon's Response   *12*
Gideon's Boldness   *14*
Gideon's Obedience   *16*

Chapter 3 – Gideon's Opposition   21
Gideon's Critics   *24*
Gideon's Detractors   *26*

Contents (cont.)

Bibliography 31

Introduction

God anoints and endows individuals with gifts and talents to serve in the Church. However, some have missed the very purpose of gifts and ministries in the Church. In the Abundant Truth Leadership Series, we will endeavor to present a proper foundation for believers to minister upon.

In this publication

In this publication, we will give a brief examination of the divine assignment and mission of the judge, Gideon. His example provides tools and instructions for those called leadership and ministry in the Church today.

THE GIDEON GUIDE

Biblical Lessons in Leadership from God's "Man of Valor"

-Chapter 1-
Gideon Self-Perception

THE GIDEON GUIDE

Biblical Lessons in Leadership from God's "Man of Valor"

THE GIDEON GUIDE

Biblical Lessons in Leadership from God's "Man of Valor"

Gideon's story is one that many are familiar with. His story reveals that all service is not behind the scenes. Many are called to lead. Hence, you have to learn the art of leadership in connection with your service to Christ.

Personal Perception

Consider Gideon: he was a man that felt like he was the least whom God chose to lead.

And he said unto him, Oh my Lord, wherewith shall I save Israel? Behold, my family is poor in

Manasseh, and I am the least in my father's house. And the LORD said unto him, Surely I will be with thee, and thou shalt smite the Midianites as one man. Judges 6:15-16 (KJV)

In spite of what he felt about himself, he was chosen to lead. Some reading this book are called to lead in the Church. Mastering the art of leadership is vital to your success.

Leadership Mandate

To lead means to direct the

operations, activity, or performance of; to guide someone or something along a way; to have charge of. We understand that leading is a great responsibility. But will we be willing to lead for the cause of Christ and the Kingdom.

As we consider leadership, Gideon's story provides 6 truths to help us master it. Read Judges, chapters 6 through 8, as we learn the art of leadership.

THE GIDEON GUIDE

Biblical Lessons in Leadership from God's "Man of Valor

THE GIDEON GUIDE
Biblical Lessons in Leadership from God's "Man of Valor"

Notes:

_____

_____

_____

_____

_____

_____

_____

_____

THE GIDEON GUIDE
Biblical Lessons in Leadership from God's "Man of Valor"

-Chapter 2-

Gideon's Example

THE GIDEON GUIDE
Biblical Lessons in Leadership from God's "Man of Valor

Gideon was the 5th Judge in Israel.

Gideon's Name

Gideon's name means Destroyer. His name signified what he was to do: Destroy the enemies of Israel.

We, too, are called to destroy the works of the enemy and build the Kingdom of God as we serve and lead.

Leadership consists of having a kingdom and Christ-centered agenda which will undermine the works of the devil in the lives of people. Christ-like leadership in service will bring men into a greater level of freedom in this life.

Gideon's Response

Let us examine Gideon's first reaction to the words of the Angel.

And Gideon said unto him, Oh my Lord, if the LORD be with us, why then is all this befallen us? and where be all his miracles which our fathers told us of, saying, Did not the LORD bring us up from Egypt? but now the LORD hath forsaken us, and delivered us into the hands of the Midianites. And the LORD looked upon him, and said, Go in this thy might, and thou shalt save Israel from the hand of the Midianites: have not I sent thee? Judges 6:13-14 (KJV)

Gideon's initial response was resistance. Sometimes we resist the command to go and lead because of our personal perspective of ourselves and life. We have to get over ourselves and our failures and respond to the challenge to lead.

If one is to lead, they must believe in Christ (who has called them) and also in their ability to fulfill what He has called them to do.

Gideon's Boldness

Gideon's gained strength and boldness as he responded to his call to lead.

He went and tore down the altar of Baal. (Judges 6:25-32)

Gideon was brave after the angelic visitation but later became afraid. At the beginning, we can be excited and eager to obey God. Yet, leadership will cause some to become fearful and afraid soon after, like Gideon.

His boldness digressed into doubt. He put out the fleece for God. However, his doubt did not lead to disobedience.

Today, we cannot allow self-doubt to push us into disobedience. Leaders are needed and God will give you what you need to do the task.

Gideon's Obedience

As we follow Gideon's story, we discover he did it God's way (Read Judges 7)

Once we have received the call to lead, make sure it is done God's way. It is the only way to ensure success. Many leaders become unfruitful in service because they rely on themselves or become self-willed. However, Gideon's story demonstrates the benefits of absolute obedience.

THE GIDEON GUIDE
Biblical Lessons in Leadership from God's "Man of Valor"

THE GIDEON GUIDE

Biblical Lessons in Leadership from God's "Man of Valor

Notes:

THE GIDEON GUIDE
Biblical Lessons in Leadership from God's "Man of Valor"

-Chapter 3-
Gideon's Opposition

From the previous chapters we can identify five vital lessons for leadership.

1. Get over yourself.

2. Trust God's choice of you.

3. God will give you what you need to lead.

4. Leading should bring men into freedom.

5. Expect opposition, accept no defeat.

THE GIDEON GUIDE

Biblical Lessons in Leadership from God's "Man of Valor"

Gideon's Critics

Gideon had to deal with criticism. The men of Ephraim wanted to be a part of the battle, but Gideon did not notify them.

Gideon was doing what he was told to do. And so, they became angry with him.

And the men of Ephraim said unto him, Why hast thou served us thus, that thou calledst us not, when thou wentest to fight with the Midianites? And they did chide with him sharply. Judges 8:1 (KJV)

We will have to deal with criticism from others we are trying to serve. Leaders face the toughest criticism from those who will benefit from their service.

Expect criticism as you lead but also expect God's peace and comfort in spite of it. The leader who forgets this will be frustrated in serving.

Gideon's Detractors Perception

Gideon had to lead without needed support. Men of Jordan would not give him and his men provision. (Read Judges 8:4-7)

As a leader, know that men may not always give you the moral and material support that you require. However, God will be faithful. If He has called you to lead, He will give you what you need, personally and provisionally, to make sure you succeed.

Gideon's story encourages us to lead, knowing that God will be with us. Therefore, go on and master the art of leadership.

THE GIDEON GUIDE
Biblical Lessons in Leadership from God's "Man of Valor"

Notes:

THE GIDEON GUIDE
Biblical Lessons in Leadership from God's "Man of Valor"

Bibliography

Smith, William. Smith's Bible Dictionary. Holman Bible Publishers. Nashville, Tennessee. c1994

The Bible Library. The Bible Library CD Rom Disc. Ellis Enterprises Incorporated, (c)1988 – 2000. 4205 McAuley Blvd., Suite 385, Oklahoma City, OK 73120. All Rights Reserved.

Lockman Foundation. Comparative Study Bible. Zondervan Publishing House. Grand Rapids, MI, c1984

THE GIDEON GUIDE

Biblical Lessons in Leadership from God's "Man of Valor

Notes:

THE GIDEON GUIDE
Biblical Lessons in Leadership from God's "Man of Valor"

www.ingramcontent.com/pod-product-compliance
Lightning Source LLC
Chambersburg PA
CBHW070241090526
44586CB00035B/1490